Badger Key S Literacy Sta___

Year 7 Sentence Level

Author: Pie Corbett

Badger Publishing Limited
26 Wedgwood Way, Pin Green Industrial Estate, Stevenage, Hertfordshire SG1 4QF
Telephone: 01438 356907. Fax: 01438 747015.

Badger Key Stage 3 Literacy Starters - Year 7 Sentence Level

First published 2001
ISBN 1 85880 863 4

Cover photograph: Educational Solutions Ltd.

Introduction

Starter activities are a dynamic way to kick off lessons with a lively start, in which all pupils are expected to contribute. The best starters are a form of linguistic gymnastics, based on the idea that the conscious manipulation of words and sentences lies at the basis of effective writing. These activities are designed to contribute to developing young writers control over language, releasing their creativity.

Key principles

The activities in this book focus on all the sentence level objectives in the national literacy strategy framework for teaching Year 7. Activities are multi sensory, using different strategies for learning such as hearing patterns; writing; memorising visually; using what is already known; developing principles, conventions, rules and mnemonics. The key principles for teaching starters are:

- They should last about 5 minutes - at the most 10.
- Activities should be fast, oral, focused and interactive.
- They are based on the notion of 'Little and Often' teaching.
- They need not be directly linked to the main teaching - though this can be helpful where links are sensible.
- They are good for breaking up longer sessions.
- They can introduce, refine, and consolidate learning - further word/sentence level teaching will be needed.

The starters in this book provide activities for:
- Developing curiosity about words/sentences;
- Introducing a pattern or convention;
- Swift investigations to help secure underlying patterns and principles;
- Revisiting and consolidating what has already been taught;
- Providing quick creative approaches to gaining an appreciation, understanding and facility with language.

Using the starters

The starters are designed to be simple to use. The teaching notes provide clear suggestions. Where relevant a photocopiable master is provided.

Experience suggests:

- You do not have to wait for everyone to finish or to check every board each time.
- You can use an edge of competition and fun.
- Differentiation is built into the activities with a 'challenge' box.
- You should watch out in case the starter takes over the main part of the lesson.
- You should aim to keep the pace going - many starters may only need to last a few minutes.
- Most activities can be carried by pairs, or small groups and benefit from rapid discussion - though they will work just as well with individuals.
- The activities are aimed at the band level 4-7.
- Finally - watch out for pupils who write messages onto the back of their white boards.

Remember all those sitting behind them can read their subversive jokes, whilst all you can see is a correct response!

Getting prepared

The teaching notes will need a quick read before the lesson. They are self - explanatory. Generally the only preparation needed is some photocopying - occasionally a PCM has to be converted into an OHT, or cards cut up for a game. Whiteboards are needed for many activities though notebooks could also be used. Coloured pens for the OHT (or classboard) and highlighters can help to draw attention to patterns. More complex terms are explained within the teaching notes, primarily for those who teach English but are not specialists.

Assessment

The class response to activities quickly reveals whether or not the majority have grasped a concept. The acid test is whether pupils can explain the reasons behind a concept, or use a language feature with ease within their own reading and writing.

End Note

Word and sentence level teaching is not primarily about gaining a degree in linguistics. It provides the knowledge and skills writers need to write effectively. Young writers who struggle with spelling, punctuation, constructing and varying sentences often find composition difficult - because too much cognitive space can be taken up with worrying over the secretarial features of writing at the expense of being able to focus upon the act of composition. Starter activities can create a buzz about words/sentences - they are a lively way of warming up language,

Sentence Level Starters

These sentence level starters are designed as mini activities that might lead into, or support, further investigations. You may wish to use them as copymasters or turn them into OHTs. Where possible, pupils should be encouraged to make links with their own specific strengths and weaknesses with sentences and words in order to develop a curiosity about language and an understanding of the strategies that will help them. In devising these activities I would like to acknowledge the researchers, teachers, writers and pupils that have helped me develop my interest in how language works.

Pie Corbett

Contents

Recapping
1. What is a sentence?
    Copymaster
2. Using adjectives and adverbs.
    Copymaster
3. Using powerful verbs.
    Copymaster
4. Varying sentence openings.
    Copymaster
5. Simple sentences for clarity.
    Copymaster
6. Compound sentences for flow.
    Copymaster
7. Complex sentences for detail.
    Copymaster
8. Using questions and exclamations.
    Copymaster

Sentence construction and punctuation.
9. Using commas.
    Copymaster
10. Creating noun phrases.
    Copymaster
11. Complex sentences.
    Copymaster
12. Sentence ambiguity.
    Copymaster
13. Varying sentences for effect (1)
    No Copymaster
14. Varying sentences for effect (2)
    No Copymaster
15. Active and passive - Who dunnit?
    Copymaster
16. Playing with tenses - Spot the error
    Copymaster
17. Using speech (1)
    Copymaster
18. Using speech (2)
    Copymaster
19. Apostrophes (1)
    No Copymaster
20. Apostrophes (2)
    No Copymaster

Paragraphing and cohesion.

21. Changing paragraphs
    Copymaster
22. Clustering ideas in a paragraph.
    Copymaster
23. Straight to the point.
    Copymaster
24. Organising a paragraph.
    Copymaster
25. Opening paragraphs.
    Copymaster
26. Varying sentences.
    Copymaster

Stylistic conventions of non-fiction.

27. Style in information texts.
    Copymaster
28. Style in recounts.
    Copymaster
29. Style in explanations.
    Copymaster
30. Style in instructions.
    Copymaster
31. Style in persuasive writing.
    Copymaster
32. Guess the style.
    Copymaster

Standard English and language variation.

33. Speech into writing.
    Copymaster
34. Using formal language.
    Copymaster
35. Standard English.
    Copymaster
36. Old and New.
    Copymaster

Writers' style.

37. Improving style - alliteration.
    No Copymaster
38. Improving style - similes.
    No Copymaster
39. Improving style - metaphors
    No Copymaster
40. Improving style - personification.
    No Copymaster

What is a sentence?

Objective:

Revise from year 6 sentence concept plus accurate construction.

Teaching point:

Create and understand sentences.

What you will need:
Copymasters, a board to write on, and a set of whiteboards.

Time:
Up to 10 minutes

Activity:

- Ask the class what makes a sentence. Begin a checklist, e.g. sentences need a capital letter, a full stop, and should 'make sense'.

- Challenge the class to write a sentence, in 10 seconds, that contains one word, e.g. poodle.

- Check the boards ~ show a few that have no capital letter or full stop (or don't make sense).

- Ask the class to try again with another word, e.g. angry. Ask them to double check ~ 'read what you have written as if you were me ~ you know what I'm looking for' (build the habit of self checking into all whiteboard work).

- Now give the word 'jelly'. Some will write a sentence using a capital 'J' in the middle ~ reinforce the notion of capital letters at the front of sentences or for special names only.

- Build up to inventing a sentence using 2, 3 or even 4 words, e.g. *shark, cry, sandwich,* e.g. *I heard a shark cry because it did not enjoy my fish paste sandwich.*

- Write up a sentence without a verb, e.g. *The dog down the lane.* What is missing? Add to definition that sentences 'have a verb'.

- Write up a sentence without a subject, e.g. *The sang sweetly.* What is missing? Add to definition that sentences 'have a subject'.

- Look at the Copymaster. Work through the first two as a class ~ pupils have to decide if it is a sentence, and give a reason.

- Play this one often to increase fundamental skill

Challenge: Find exceptions, e.g. Silence! Discuss use of implied verb.

What has been taught:
- A sentence needs a capital letter, a full stop, generally contains a verb and a subject, and 'makes sense'.

What is a sentence?

Read these sentences through ~ tick the box to show if it is a sentence or not ~ and give a reason.

1. Mad old Mrs Maltravers the cows down the back lane. ☐

2. The painted the caravan a fresh green colour. ☐

3. Chocolate doughnuts should be given all pupils. ☐

4. Smoking dangerous. ☐

5. Sharks, snakes and wolves are feared by. ☐

6. E-mail is a great way to communicate but have to be careful of sending each other a virus. ☐

7. When we to Spain I saw a Gecko. ☐

8. Turn the handle to the left. ☐

9. Pollution is the main cause of. ☐

Using adjectives and adverbs

Objective:

Revise from year 6 use of adverbs and adjectives.

Teaching point:

Adjectives and adverbs must be used with care.

What you will need:
Copymasters, a board, 4 coloured markers, and whiteboards.

Time:
Up to 10 minutes

Activity:

• Write up a dull sentence, e.g. *The dog barked*. Insert an adjective.

• What is an adjective? Start checklist ~ it describes a noun, tells the reader more information, helps to build a stronger picture, etc.

• Underline the noun in one colour and the adjective in another colour. Do they always go together?

• Write up: 'The car was red.' Is there an adjective? It is an adjective because it describes the noun (add point to checklist).

• Class make up a sentence using 2, 3, 4 adjectives to a noun. Does it sound good? Add 'don't use lots of adjectives/choose with care'.

• Carry out the same activity with adverbs ~ use the same sentence: 'The dog barked.' Note how the adverb tells us more about the verb. Using too many sounds silly. Adverbs are very mobile, e.g. '*The dog barked mournfully*' or '*Mournfully, the dog barked*' or '*The dog mournfully barked*'.

• Practise moving adverbs around in a sentence, e.g. The girls opened the door from the kitchen, cautiously.

• The copymaster looks at selecting adjectives and adverbs carefully.

Check that invented sentences have a capital letter, etc. Discuss choice of adverb/adjective.

Challenge: Collect adverbs that tell the reader how (slowly), where (there), or when (yesterday) things happened.

What has been taught:
• An adjective is a word that describes somebody, or something.
• An adverb also gives extra meaning, usually to a verb.
• Practise in skill of selecting carefully and moving adjectives and adverbs.

Underline adjectives. Write a comment chosen from the comment box.

1. The big giant crushed the house.

2. The slim, silver, shining, flickering, brilliant, sleek salmon swam.

3. The tired and weary cat slept.

4. The rusty key was rusty.

5. The hot ice cream was served.

Underline the adverbs. Write a comment from the comment box.

1. The choir sang sweetly, precisely, loudly, amazingly.

2. The cat snored loudly and noisily

3. Silently, Solly crept down the path silently.

4. The massive bomb exploded loudly.

5. The shy clown wept.

Comment Box:
  - too many
  - mean the same
  - too obvious
  - repetition
  - adds something new

Using powerful verbs

Objective:
Revise from year 6 the use of verbs.

Teaching point:
A verb describes actions and must be selected with care.

What you will need:
A board to write on, set of whiteboards, OHT and pen.

Time:
Up to 10 minutes

Activity:

- What is a verb? Make a checklist ~ most will suggest that it is a 'doing' word, it describes what happens, etc.

- Write up: 'The cat scratched the dog.' Pupils write down the verb.

- Write up: 'The cat was red.' Which is the verb? Tease out that a verb describes actions or a 'state of being' ~ how we are.

- Write up: 'The cat would have scratched the dog.' Which is the verb? Explain that sometimes the verb is made up of more than one word, e.g. The cat was purring.

- Use OHT. Cover all the sentences and reveal one at a time.

- Pupils jot on whiteboard the verb or verb chain. They then select a more powerful verb. Alter sentence on OHT and discuss impact.

- Discuss the impact of different choices, e.g.

  'The Queen ate the bun.' ~ doesn't tell the reader much.

  'The Queen scoffed the bun.' ~ suggests she might be hungry or the bun might be exceptionally tasty.

  'The Queen nibbled the bun.' ~ suggests she might be feeling full or ill, or the bun might look rather unpleasant!

Check that class can identify the verb, and can think of more powerful alternatives.

Challenge: In 2 minutes list as many alternatives for ~ went, ate, look, said. Who can list the most?

What has been taught:
- A verb describes an action or state of being.
- Powerful verbs add extra meaning to a sentence, for instance about character.

Using powerful verbs

Which is the verb? Select more powerful verbs.

1. The Queen ate the bun.

2. The Prime Minister went all the way round the M25 for charity.

3. The robber looked into the jeweller's window at the diamond rings.

4. Slim Dragwort got out of the Mercedes.

5. "No!" said Ariadne Dragwort.

6. As he moved down the wall, Slim got the rope and held on.

7. The hippo went past the front entrance and laughed.

8. Fortunately, the zoo keeper got the hippo with an iced bun.

9. Mrs Dragwort looked at the scruffy boy.

10. Idly, Slim moved over to the hippo and said the password.

Varying sentence openings

Objective:
Revise sentence variation from year 6.

Teaching point:
Starting sentences in the same way can make your writing dull ~ there are various way to vary the opening of a sentence. Revisit this idea often ~ discussing how writers use these tactics, asking children to improve sections of their writing by varying the openings.

What you will need:
A board to write on, a class set of whiteboards and OHT.

Time:
5 - 10 minutes

Activity:

• Read the top passage on the OHT. What do you notice? All the sentences sound similar, start in the same way, sound dull, etc.

• Go through the 6 sentences on the OHT, identifying how the openings have been varied. For each one, imitate the pattern several times, e.g.

Slowly, the old man woke up.

Angrily, the doctor stabbed in the needle.

Busily, the nurse tidied up the mess.

• End by rewriting the passage as a class, varying the openings.

Check that commas have been used correctly.

Challenge: How many different ways can this sentence be written?
Solly ran like the wind, across the park, rushing towards the gate, laughing madly.

What has been taught:
• Six strategies for varying the openings of sentences ~ encourage children to use this in their writing.

He crept up to the door. He opened the door. He held the dog by the collar. He stepped into the room. The light startled him. He could not see much. He could just see the dim outline of Mr Cringe. He dived back through the door.

1. Slowly, the old man woke up.

2. Running as hard as he could, Mac made it to the cave.

3. Startled by the noise, Solly spun round.

4. In the corner stood an old crystal mirror.

5. Although he was thirsty, Mac refused to drink the potion.

6. Quick as a knife, he stabbed his finger at the button.

To vary sentence openings: simile, connective, adverb, prepositional phrase, 'ed' or 'ing' word.

Simple sentences for clarity

Objective:
Revise from year 6 simple sentences.

Teaching point:
Simple sentences are useful for clarity, emphasis and drama.

What you will need:
Copymasters, a board to write on, and a class set of whiteboards.

Time:
5 minutes

Activity:

- Write up the following sentence: - 'The cat purred.'

- Explain it is a 'simple' sentence ~ with one verb and one subject.

- Which is the verb?

- Which is the subject ~ the word that the sentence is about?

- Challenge the children to make the sentence much longer but there must only be one subject and one verb, e.g. The one-eyed, wild, tabby cat purred all through the morning.

- Class now rapidly invent simple sentences with you supplying the verb (swam, picked, carried, held, sneezed) or the subject (dog, fish, gun, foot, nail) or both (phone/rang, pool/froze, computer/exploded).

- Class work on the copymasters ~ look at the first sentence. Demonstrate how to underline the verb and circle the subject.

- They underline and circle in the next four sentences.

- Then they have to rewrite the final lengthy sentences as simple sentences to make them either: clearer so that the reader can simply understand; more dramatic; or more emphatic ~ drumming home a point.

Check that everyone is still writing 'proper' sentences.

Challenge: Skim their class reader and find a simple sentence ~ is it for clarity, emphasis or drama?

What has been taught:
- In a simple sentence there is only one verb and one subject. The subject carries out the action. Simple sentences are useful for clarity, drama and emphasis.

Simple sentences for clarity

Circle the subject and underline the verb.

1. The lorry slid down the hill.

2. Tarzan swooped through the jungle at great speed.

3. Billie grabbed the metal bars of the rusted gate.

4. In the afternoon she drank a whole pint of milk.

5. Later that day Timo told Tarzan the truth.

Rewrite as 2 simple sentences ~ for clarity, drama and emphasis.

With a noise that could have awoken the dead, and before anyone could speak, the blue and white wooden door closed behind them, shuddering and making the walls shake. At that terrible moment they realised that despite everything that they had tried it all now came down to this one terrible realisation that they were trapped through their own stupidity and carelessness.

Compound sentences for flow

Objective:

Revise compound sentences from year 6.

Teaching point:

Compound sentences are useful for 'flow' when writing.

What you will need:
Copymasters and a set
of whiteboards.

Time:
5 - 10 minutes

Activity:

• On the copymaster join the pairs of simple sentences together using *and*, *but* or *or*.

• Discuss reasons why it improves the writing.

• Rewrite the first paragraph (B) of simple sentences using some compound sentences to help the writing flow more easily.
  Beware ~ don't overdo it!

• Revise the second paragraph (C) where the use of 'and' has gone into overdrive!

Check whether when joining simple sentences the subject (and sometimes the repeated verb) can be removed. Are sentences demarcated correctly? Insist that re-reading is used to check 'how it sounds'.

Challenge: Write a short paragraph about a subject you know well, using this pattern:
  • Simple sentence.
  • Compound sentences.
  • Simple sentence.
  Starting and ending a paragraph with a simple sentence can help to clarify your writing.

What has been taught:
  • Compound sentences can help writing read more easily.

Compound sentences for flow

A. Join these pairs of simple sentences together ~ use *and, but* or *or.* You may slightly alter the sentences if need be.

Explain why it improves the writing.

1. Plants need water. Plants need sunshine.

2. He crossed the road. He went down to the shops.

3. Smoking is dangerous. Many people ignore the warnings.

4. The sea is often cold. Some people swim in it.

5. You can go to the swimming pool. You can go to the cinema.

6. In Spain the weather is hot. It can be cold in Winter.

B. Timo went into the shop. He looked at the cameras. He liked the look of one. It had no proper case. He noticed one with a zoom lens. It had a built in flash. He had to make his mind up. It would be too late.

C. Shelly rushed into the classroom and began to shout and Skiver joined in and made a fantastic whooping noise and at that moment Mr Cringe strode in and roared at everyone and there was silence.

Complex sentences for detail

Objective:

Revise complex sentences from year 6.

Teaching point:

Complex sentences help a writer add in extra layers of meaning.

What you will need:
OHT.

Time:
5 - 10 minutes

Activity:

- Use the OHT to show the first sentence and the list of connectives. Demonstrate how the basic sentence could have further detail added to it by using a subordinate clause either before or after the main clause, e.g.

  Main clause: Jo grabbed the tightrope.

  Before: As the crowd roared, Jo grabbed the tightrope.

  After: Jo grabbed the tightrope because she was afraid.

- The class take each sentence in turn and use a connective to create a subordinate clause either before or after the main clause.

Check that where the subordinate clause precedes the main clause it is followed by a comma, e.g. Although I am tired, I pressed on.

Challenge: Create a sentence that uses a subordinate clause before and after the main clause. Think about where the commas should go.

What has been taught:
- Subordinate clauses can help writers add in extra information or detail.

Complex sentences for detail

Jo grabbed the tightrope.

Before:

After:

Choose a connective: because, whenever, despite, even though, however, although, whilst, until, before, since, as, after, whereas, unless.

1. It was a rattlesnake.

2. The lizard's head nodded.

3. I ran to the car.

4. Dolphins are intelligent.

5. Wasps sting.

6. Driving fast is against the law.

Using questions and exclamations

Objective:
Revise sentence types from year 6.

Teaching point:
Questions and exclamations help to vary writing.

What you will need:
Whiteboards and a board to write on.

Time:
5 - 10 minutes

Activity:

- Look at the 4 sentences on the OHT. Write on your whiteboard the type they are.

  Question ~ usually needs a reply.

  Statement ~ states facts or opinions.

  Command ~ is an order.

  Exclamation ~ expresses surprise or emotion or a warning.

- Write up a list of 3 or 4 subjects (moon, mirror, key, secret). Build 4 sentences, one of each type around the subjects. Do the first as a class, e.g.

  Question ~ Why did you get that silvery glow?

  Statement ~ The moon lights up the darkness.

  Command ~ Hide your face behind a cloud.

  Exclamation ~ Blink!

Check that sentences are accurate ~ highlight interesting ideas.

Challenge: Write a question and answer poem.

What has been taught:
- There are four basic types of sentence that vary writing.

Turn the handle to the right.

Run for it!

Frogs like still water.

Where have you hidden the message?

Using commas

Objective: S3

Use punctuation to clarify meaning, particularly at the boundaries between sentences and clauses.

Teaching point:

Commas are used with certain grammatical constructions.

What you will need:
Copymasters and whiteboards.

Time:
5 - 10 minutes

Activity:

- Read through the sentences, noting the reason for a comma.

- On a board imitate each one, e.g.

  Blueberry, singing at the top of his voice, sauntered down the track.

  Sasha, rushing to the bus stop, tripped over.

- The class imitate each one on their whiteboards.

Check that the class reread and check for punctuation and sense before holding their sentence up.

Challenge: Find an example of each in class reader ~ add to invented sentence on whiteboard.

What has been taught:
- Commas are used with a number of grammatical constructions.

Imitate each sentence, using commas.

1. Blueberry, singing at the top of his voice, sauntered down the track.

2. Cunningly, the fox opened its mouth to speak.

3. Before electricity was available, many people died of cold in the winter.

4. Pausing to check the timer, Bragger slipped and fell.

5. 'Daisy, come over here.'

6. 'You won't be all day, will you?'

7. He said, 'Is that a salamander that you have under your hat?'

Key:
1. Drop in a clause.
2. Start with an adverb.
3. Start with a subordinate clause.
4. Start with 'ed' or 'ing' word.
5. Address someone else.
6. Tag on a question.
7. Speech.

Creating noun phrases

Objective: S2

Expand nouns and noun phrases, e.g. *by using a prepositional phrase.*

Teaching point:

Nouns can be made more precise and vivid by creating noun phrases.

What you will need:
A board to write on, whiteboards or notebooks and copymasters.

Time:
5 - 10 minutes

Activity:

- Write up a simple sentence, e.g. **The girl laughed at the clown.**

- Underline each noun and then demonstrate how each one could be expanded, e.g. **The red haired girl by the station wagon laughed at the daft clown who wept.**

- Explain how there are two possibilities ~ words before the noun and words after the noun.

- Build a noun tower, adding extra bits on each time, to a noun from a sentence (**The dogs are a nuisance**), e.g.
  Dogs
  Those dogs
  Those white dogs
  Those white, savage dogs
  Those white, savage dogs in the road
  Those white, savage dogs in the road growling at me

- Provide a series of questions to steer the noun towers, e.g.
  - Which ones (determiners) ~ my, the, all, some, those, this, that, a, many, every, etc.
  - What are they like (adjectives) ~ green, spotted, large, cruel, rusty, slim, etc.
  - Where (prepositional phrase) ~ by the road, behind the garage, etc.
  - Doing what (clause) ~ running away, seated neatly, who was scared, that I'd noticed, etc.

- On the copymasters there are 5 sentences with a noun in, each underlined. The task is to create noun towers, e.g. **cat, car, boy, girl, ice-cream.**

Check that noun phrases are created.

Challenge: Create noun phrases for the other nouns.

What has been taught:
- Nouns can be built up to create more vivid descriptions for the reader.

1. The <u>cat</u> ate the bone.

2. The <u>car</u> raced towards the city.

3. The <u>boy</u> ran to the shop.

4. The <u>girl</u> kicked at her attacker.

5. The <u>ice-cream</u> melted onto the ground.

Complex sentences

Objective: S1

Deploying subordinate clauses in a variety of positions within the sentence.

Teaching point:

You can drop a subordinate clause into a sentence, adding in an extra layer of information.

What you will need:
OHT.

Time:
5 - 10 minutes

Activity:

- Use the OHT to show how a sentence can be expanded by inserting a subordinate clause.

- Draw their attention to the options for starting the clause.

- The task is to drop a clause into each of the sentences, selecting an appropriate word from the options box.

Check that commas are used to cordon off the clause.

Challenge: Complete all sentences.

What has been taught:
- To drop a subordinate clause into a sentence.

Complex sentences

The carrot is stale.

The carrot, that was left over, is stale.

> **Options box:**
> who, which, whose, where, when, that.

1. Basil Fawlty thrashed his car.

2. The Mercedes bumped down the street.

3. The knife was sharp.

4. On Friday we will feed the monkeys.

5. In Spain they sleep in the afternoon.

6. Melissa turned up at school wearing jeans.

Sentence ambiguity

Objective: S6

Recognise and remedy ambiguity in sentences, e.g. unclear use of pronouns.

Teaching point:

As you are writing and after you have finished always reread as if you were the reader, checking to see if your writing is clear.

What you will need:
Copymasters and a class set of whiteboards.

Time:
5 - 10 minutes

Activity:

• Read through the sentences on the copymasters.

• On whiteboards the class rewrite each one solving the confusion.

• Discuss how the different confusions arise.

Check that use of pronouns is clear, as this is where most errors occur in pupils' writing.

Challenge: Write other 'for sale' of 'wanted' signs that involve ambiguity.

What has been taught:
• Sentences can become muddled unless it is clear to whom pronouns refer. Furthermore - parts of sentences about the same thing need to be kept together.

1. Tom had walked for miles to speak to Sam. He was hungry as a horse.

2. Kylie rushed to the shops to buy a present and then took it round to see Jo who was working hard. She was tired.

3. I spoke to a man looking at a box with a fur lined bottom.

4. I saw Mrs Cringe holding a comb with plastic teeth.

5. Wanted: Elephant for bored millionaire with long tusks.

6. For sale: Pyramids for pharaoh with pointed top.

Varying sentences for effect (1)

Objective: S11

Vary the structure of sentences within paragraphs to lend pace, variety and emphasis.

Teaching point:

Sentence structure needs to be adapted according to audience and purpose.

What you will need:
A class set
of whiteboards.

Time:
As required

Activity:

- Provide a basic sentence, e.g. Jo made a jam butty.

- On whiteboards the class have to rewrite the sentence to make it fit into:
  - a newspaper headline (Jam Butty Breakthrough);
  - a story (Carefully, Jo spread the jam);
  - a poem (Like seeds of blood the jam spread);
  - an information book (Bread can be spread with many different preserves, jam being the most popular);
  - an advert (Spread the rumour ~ spread jam);
  - a diary (The jam butties were brill);
  - a letter of complaint (The jam sandwiches were disgusting…);
  - a set of instructions (First, spread the jam evenly…);
  - dramatic (The deadly jam spread);
  - descriptive (the red, sweet jam, like a smear of blood, spread evenly);
  - speech question ('Spread the toast will you?')
  - for younger children (Spread the jam on the bread), etc.

- The game can be played by just providing a word for transformation.

This is a simple game that can be played on many occasions. It can be as swift as you like ~ possibly just used as a mental warm up for a couple of minutes.

Check that the class reread to check for accuracy and sense. Draw attention to sentences that do sound like the different text types.

Challenge: A pair of pupils draw up the basic sentence and list of instructions, running the game themselves. Try using two related sentences.

What has been taught:
- Swiftly adapting sentences for different purposes.

Varying sentences for effect (2)

Objective: S1

Revise extending sentences to add variation from year 6.

What you will need:
A class set of whiteboards and a board to write on.

Time:
2 - 10 minutes

Teaching point:

Sentences can be extended in a variety of ways to add in extra information or detail.

Activity:

- Write up a very short sentence, e.g. 'The worm wriggled.' The class have to make this more interesting by extending the sentence in some way.
They could try the following:

- Add in an adjective, 'The slim worm wriggled.'

- Add in an adverb, 'The worm wriggled crazily.'

- Add more onto the end of the sentence, 'The worm wriggled until it was out of breath.'

- Add more onto the front of the sentence, 'Although it was tired, the worm wriggled.'

- Any combination of the above.

- Ask the class to use different connectives, e.g. although, but, when, because, however, as, after, before, since, though, until, unless, whenever, etc.

Check that the sentences have a capital letter, full stop and make sense. Highlight good use of adjectives, adverbs or verbs plus anything unusual or interesting.

Challenge: Introduce the idea of the 'prepositional phrase' which tells us 'where' things happened, e.g. at the end of the lane, in the house, over the hill, beside the pool, etc. Practise extending sentences in this way, investigating where such phrases can be added, e.g. Into the earth, the worm wriggled.
The worm wriggled into the earth.

What has been taught:
- Sentences can be extended by adding the words into, or onto, them.

Active and passive ~ Who dunnit?

Objective: S5

Use the active and passive voice to suit purpose.

Teaching point:

Learning to use the passive.

What you will need:
Copymasters and a class set of whiteboards.

Time:
5 - 10 minutes

Activity:

- Use the copymasters to play a simple game of 'who dunnit'. The sentences are all in the passive voice, hiding the subject ~ the perpetrator of the actions.

- The task is to extend the sentences using the word 'by' and adding in the name of the perpetrator. Then in the plenary convert orally from passive to active.

- Demonstrate how to convert the first back to active, e.g.

  Grandma was eaten alive <u>by the wolf</u>.

  The wolf ate Grandma alive.

Check that most can convert passive back to active.

Challenge: Early finishers can invent several more in passive voice for the rest of the class to guess.

What has been taught:
- Passive voice can be used when the subject is not needed, you are uncertain who the subject might be or you wish to hide the subject.

Active and passive ~ Who dunnit?

Sentences are written in the passive when you do not need to know, or you are uncertain, who did something, e.g.

A scientist might write ~ The chemicals were heated.

A reporter might write - The road was cleared.

A historian might write ~ Stones were brought to Stone Henge.

A child might say ~ Mum, the mirror's been broken.

These sentences are in the passive to hide 'who dunnit'. Complete each one using the word 'by' ~ the first is done for you.

1. Grandma was eaten alive *by the wolf.*

2. 3 chairs and 3 beds were smashed . . . .

3. An apple was shot from a boy's head . . . .

4. Wealthy merchants have been robbed to feed the poor . . . .

. . . .

5. A troll was thrown into the water . . . .

6. A lost boy was cared for . . . .

7. Golden eggs were stolen . . . .

8. A glass slipper has been left behind . . . .

9. Young girls was rescued from a tower . . . .

10. A small, flying golden ball was caught mid air . . . .

Playing with tenses ~ Spot the error

Objective: S4

Keep tense usage consistent, and manage changes of tense so that meaning is clear.

Teaching point:

It is important to keep in the same tense and to ensure that you use the correct spelling.

What you will need:
OHT and a class set of whiteboards.

Time:
5 minutes

Activity:

- Read through the passages (A1 and A2) at the top of the OHT. What is the difference (one is in the past and one in the present)?
  How did you know ~ which words told you?

- Use the sentences (B), possible openings to narrative, on the rest of the OHT to play 'improve' ~ pupils read through and make a list of alterations. This should only take a few minutes.

Check that correct spelling is used.

Challenge: Early finishers should rewrite number 9 and be prepared to explain why it is not only the verb that is not in standard form.

What has been taught:
- To identify inappropriate shifts in tense and correct them.

Playing with tenses ~ Spot the error

A1 Bracewater backed the car up to the bank. He slammed on the brakes and leaped out. The newspaper seller across the road lowered his sunglasses and muttered something into a mobile phone. Bracewater marched towards the bank's doors. Unfortunately, it was 8 o'clock ~ locked!

A2 Bracewater backs the car up to the bank. He slams on the brakes and leaps out. The newspaper seller across the road lowers his sunglasses and mutters something into a mobile phone. Bracewater marches towards the bank's doors. Unfortunately, it is 8 o'clock ~ locked!

B 1. The sunlight streamed onto the prison floor where Bracewater sleeps.

2. The scurge of Gloucester, Skadell, opens one eye and watched a fly settle on his tail.

3. Sandi Dawson sneezed, picks up his packed lunch and dashed out to catch the bus.

4. Shelley knew all about bullies, and she were determined to win.

5. Just beyond the galaxy Zargrab spinned the mighty star Cornrunner, where the Hunter lived in splendid isolation.

6. Corrin grinned at himself and tooked a swig of tea.

7. Outside the wind howled, snow piled up against the back door and a shadow were limping down from the forest.

8. Skarla was dead frit of wolves.

Using speech (1)

Objective: S7

Use speech punctuation accurately to integrate speech into larger sentences.

Teaching point:

You can break a string of speech up by describing what the speaker did.

What you will need:
Copymasters.

Time:
10 minutes

Activity:

- Look at copymasters together. What is wrong with the first section of dialogue? (It's hard to tell who is speaking ~ you cannot really see in your mind what is happening ~ it's dull, etc.)

- Explain that the focus is upon looking at one way to begin to break up a string of speech and improve dialogue writing.

- Notice how in the second example what is said is followed by a description of what the speaker did as she spoke.

- How is Mrs Ramsbotham feeling? Make the point that the accompanying action shows the reader how the character feels. Characteristaion comes through what characters say and do.

- Make the sentence pattern clear, e.g. write down the words spoken; write she/he said; use a comma; describe what the speaker did, leading into this with a verb ending in 'ing' or 'ed'.

- Invent an example together, e.g.
  "Clear off," muttered Sal, picking up her glasses and staring at the mouse.

- The task is to take the next three pairs of dialogue and to insert what the speaker does at the end of the first part of the conversation.

- Think about how the character might be feeling. Make the action reflect in some way the sort of thing that someone who feels that way might do.

- Make the point that if you keep doing this it will sound odd ~ but it is one useful tactic.

Check that accurate punctuation is used.

Challenge: Try to improve the initial string of dialogue.

What has been taught:
- A string of endless speech can be broken by describing what the speaker is doing. This in turn can help to build up the character.

"Hello."
"Hi."
"Ok."
"Well."
"Hi."
"Hi."

"The donuts are ready to eat", said Mrs Ramsbotham, grinning at her family as she placed the dish on the table with a flourish.

"Get out," snarled Jazz.

"Keep your hair on," retorted Brand.

"Dad, can we go down the canal," asked Jo.

"I've told you before and the answer hasn't changed," replied Mr Cotterill.

"I thought that you ought to know," said Sandi.

"Thanks a bunch," muttered her sister.

Using speech (2)

Objective: S7

Use speech punctuation accurately to integrate speech into larger sentences.

What you will need:
Copymasters plus a set of whiteboards.

Time:
10 minutes

Teaching point:

To break up a string of speech you can not only describe what the speaker is doing (see unit 18) but also add in the listener's reactions and anything else that is happening.

Activity:

• Notice how the first piece of dialogue runs the risk of becoming a string of speech. It does not help the reader picture what is happening, merely reports what was said.

• In the second piece of dialogue what Mrs Ramsbotham did has been added, using the strategy taught in the previous unit. But then we see her husband's reaction.

• Once again the listener's reaction should reflect what they feel.

• Model rewriting the third piece of dialogue, featuring Jazz and Brand, e.g.

"Get out," snarled Jazz, startled by Brand bursting into her room. Brand paused long enough to notice that she was writing a letter. A letter to their mother.
"Keep your hair on," he retorted.

• The class now rewrite the final two sections of dialogue in the same way.

Check that basic speech punctuation remains accurate and that what the characters do suggests how they feel.

Challenge: Continue the dialogue.

What has been taught:
• Dialogue can be improved by describing
- what the speaker does;
- what the listener does.

"The donuts are ready to eat", said Mrs Ramsbotham.
"Oh no, not more donuts," sighed Mr Ramsbotham.

"The donuts are ready to eat", said Mrs Ramsbotham, grinning at her family as she placed the dish on the table with a flourish. Mr Ramsbotham glanced up from his newspaper and winced.
"Oh no, not more donuts," he sighed.

"Get out," snarled Jazz.

"Keep your hair on," retorted Brand.

"Dad, can we go down the canal," asked Jo.

"I've told you before and the answer hasn't changed," replied Mr Cotterill.

"I thought that you ought to know," said Sandi.

"Thanks a bunch," muttered her sister.

Apostrophes (1)

Objective: S3

Use punctuation to clarify meaning.

What you will need:
A class set
of whiteboards.

Time:
As you require

Teaching point:

Apostrophes should be used to show where some letters have
been missed out.

Activity:

- Explain that apostrophes began as a way of showing that certain letters had been
  omitted, e.g. Don't = do not.

- To reinforce this notion call out a contracted form and the class jot down the equation,
  e.g. should've = should have. Rather than stretching this out in one session it might be
  better to return to it as a quick-fire activity over a number of weeks ~ just to reinforce,
  remind and consolidate. Possible contenders include:

  Don't, won't, can't, shan't, she's, he's, they've, we've, hasn't, there's, mustn't, I'm,
  let's, she'd, he'd, we'd, we're, you're, we'll, they'll, she'll, he'll, I've, you've,
  should've could've, might've, it's.

- Write a few pieces of dialogue using words from the above list ~ make the point that
  generally this is used in informal writing and dialogue.

Check that the apostrophe is in the right place.

Challenge: Collect other instances where letters have been omitted,
e.g. o'clock (of the clock).

What has been taught:
- Apostrophes are used to show where letters have been missed out.

Apostrophes (2)

Objective: S3

Use punctuation to clarify meaning.

Teaching point:

Apostrophes used to show to show possession.

What you will need:
A class set
of whiteboards.

Time:
As you require

Activity:

- Apostrophes for possession can be more problematic than omission because it does require a conceptual understanding. Try a similar tactic to the previous unit idea. Say a sentence in which an apostrophe for possession will be used (at first stay with singular nouns). The class writes down the equation in this way:

Initial sentence:

It is the cat's dinner.
Cat's = belongs to the cat.

- Eventually move onto sentences that use numbers to make it obvious that you are using a plural:

Initial sentence:

The two boys' boots were ruined.
Boys' = belongs to the boys

- Try writing sentences using apostrophes for possession. This could be built around the teacher asking questions, e.g. Whose pen is it? The pupils write down the answer, e.g. It is Tim's pen.

Check that the apostrophe is in the right place.

Reminder: theirs, ours and its do not have apostrophes for possession.

Challenge: Be on the lookout for instances in shop displays, etc where the apostrophe is used incorrectly, e.g. FRESH EGG'S

What has been taught:
- Apostrophes are used to show possession.

Changing paragraphs

Objective: S8

Recognise the cues to start a new paragraph and use the first sentence effectively to orientate the reader, e.g. when there is a shift of topic, viewpoint or time.

Teaching point:

Key reasons why writers change paragraphs in narrative

What you will need:
OHT.

Time:
5 - 10 minutes

Activity:

- Why do we change paragraph in story writing? Start a list.

- Look at the OHT where there are 10 different openings to narrative paragraphs.

- The task is to write on the whiteboard a reason for changing paragraph ~ give, say, a couple of minutes for this ~ perhaps making it like a race, with the class divided into small groups.

- Discuss as a class the different reasons and complete the class list.

Check that the list created is then used to guide pupils' own writing and referred to in reading.

Challenge: First to finish could earn extra points by inventing alternative openings to paragraphs, under the same categories.

What has been taught:
- Writers change paragraph in narrative for 5 main reasons ~ change of speaker, time, place, event, viewpoint or for a particular effect (introducing tension or a dilemma).

Changing paragraphs

There was an almighty crash.

"No," replied Fred.

Mrs Tompkins eyed her daughter and wondered what on earth she was up to.

"If that is your wish," said Mr Grainger.

Back in Winklestom, the fog was so thick that even the streets had become unsure of themselves.

While Bill seemed happy, Lara was not because she had hope to reach the outpost that same day.

Later that afternoon, the goldfish wandered into town.

Suddenly, the car stopped.

On the other side of the town the Pazz was getting ready to hit the town.

It was not until early the next morning that Mrs Petersham discovered that she had lost the poodle.

Clustering ideas in a paragraph

Objective:
Revise from year 6 how in non-fiction ideas are grouped together in paragraphs.

Teaching point:
Openings, endings and clustering points together within paragraphs.

What you will need:
Copymasters.

Time:
5 - 10 minutes

Activity:

• Look at the copymaster - on the left hand side is a list of points about living in a town. Down the right hand side the writer has clustered the points needed for the introduction. At the bottom of the copymaster you can see the opening paragraph.

• The task is to cluster the points from the list under the other relevant paragraph headings.

Check that points are clustered under the right headings.

Challenge: Write one of the paragraphs, using the points clustered and adding others. Find a topic sentence to start the paragraph, that signals to the reader what it is about.

What has been taught:
• In non-fiction each paragraph acts as a large unit of meaning, with relevant points clustered together. The tactic of planning non-fiction by thinking about an introduction (introducing the reader to the topic), an ending (often relating the subject in some personal way to the reader) with paragraphs that cluster points relating to the same aspect together in between is an important foundation.

Clustering ideas in a paragraph

Need to explore advantages
Near shops
Noisy
Near park
Mention disadvantages
Pollution
Near cinema
Plenty of choice
High rate of crime
Compare to countryside
Easy to meet people
Can't go out so much on your own
More amenities
Might get mugged
Make a personal conclusion.
Near skateboard park, swimming pool.
Wouldn't know most people
Easy to catch train

Introduction ~ town life.

- explore
  advantages/disadvantages;

- comparison with countryside;

- draw a personal conclusion.

Good reasons.

Disadvantages

Is town life all that it is meant to be cracked up? There are many
advantages to living in the town but also, some disadvantages.
Before drawing any conclusions it is important to compare town
and country life, looking at the topic from both sides.

Straight to the point

Objective: S9

Identify the main point in a paragraph, and how the supporting information relates to it, e.g. *as illustration*.

Teaching point:

In non fiction paragraphs are usually built around one main point, or topic, that is then illustrated with examples or supported by detail or argument. Typically, a paragraph includes a 'topic sentence' which contains the theme of the paragraph.

What you will need:
Copymasters.

Time:
5 - 10 minutes

Activity:

• Read through the copymaster ~ the task is to identify and underline the key point in each paragraph.

• Once completed discuss how in most paragraphs the topic sentence contains the main idea or theme.

• This usually comes at the start of the paragraph, introducing the key idea and is followed by supporting points.

• However, it can fall at the end, summarising the points made.

Challenge: Use any sample of non-fiction and identify where the topic sentences typically come ~ first, last or elsewhere?

What has been taught:
• Usually, one sentence in a paragraph contains the key idea.

Straight to the point

Sharks are some of the most feared creatures on this planet. Many people are disturbed when they swim because they fear that a shark will bite their legs. This fear has been made worse by such films as 'Jaws', which featured frightening images of swimmers being killed by sharks. Even when people are swimming in places where sharks are unknown they still feel afraid.

In this country there are no poisonous spiders. They do have a small amount of poison which they use to stun or kill their prey. In the main spiders live off other very small insects that they catch in their webs. These webs are useful to have in a house because they trap flies, mosquitoes, midges and even wasps. Spiders are a free and simple way to keep down such unwanted intruders. So, it can be seen that spiders do more good than harm.

Scorpions live in warm dry climates. They may be small but they can pack a punch. The sting of a scorpion is highly poisonous and could kill a young child, old or sick person. They use the sting to kill their prey which they grab with their pincers. In the main they hunt at night. So, if you are on holiday in a warm country just watch your step late at night if you are walking about!

Year 7 Sentence level Starter 24
Organising a paragraph

Objective: S10

Recognise how sentences are organised in a paragraph in which the content is not chronological, e.g. *by comparison*.

Teaching point:

When paragraphs are not ordered chronologically, they still must contain a logical order.

What you will need:
Copymasters.

Time:
10 minutes

Activity:

- Re-sort the sentences to create a logical paragraph.

- Remind the class to look for the topic sentence that introduces the paragraph, setting the scene.

- As they reassemble, they should keep re-reading to check whether the order is logical.

Challenge: Carry out as a 'speed test' ~ giving only a limited number of minutes to complete.

What has been taught:
- This sort of activity helps pupils to internalise the pattern of non-chronological writing.

Organising a paragraph

This paragraph is muddled. Sort the sentences out until they are in the right order.

In fact, domestic dogs are all descended from the grey wolf.

Most of us think of dogs as pets but across the world there are many different kinds of wild dog.

Of all the dogs, the wolf is the best known and the most feared by man.

So that sleepy pooch, lying on the carpet at home, is a distant relative of one of the most feared creatures alive.

This includes 2 kinds of wolves, 21 kinds of foxes and four types of jackal.

So many stories and films have featured wolves as killers that the poor animal hardly stands a chance.

Opening paragraphs

Objective: S12

Organise ideas into a coherent sequence of paragraphs, introducing, developing and concluding them appropriately.

Teaching point:

This activity focuses upon connectives and useful topic sentences to start a non-fiction paragraph.

What you will need:
Copymasters.

Time:
5 - 10 minutes

Activity:

- On the copymaster there is a list of 10 sentences.

- The class has to grade the sentences ~ according to which would make a good topic sentence to introduce a non-fiction paragraph.

- They should underline the connective that indicates the function of the sentence, e.g. to introduce, conclude, explain, list, reinforce, indicate time, etc.

- The best will have the highest scores.

Challenge: take the best and worst - jot down an explanation. Why does this sentence work/not work as an introductory sentence for a paragraph.

What has been taught:
- topic sentences can:
  - pose a question that is then explored;
  - make a statement that will then be supported;
  - make a generalisation that is then given detailed backing;
  - set out an initial proposition;
  - provide a viewpoint that is then supported or refuted, etc.

Opening paragraphs

Which of these would work well as opening sentences to a paragraph? Give a score out of 10 to each sentence, with 10 showing the most successful.

1. In short, vampires do not exist.

2. For example, it is more dangerous to travel by road than by train.

3. Starting at a new school is one of the biggest changes anyone ever makes.

4. First of all, it is against the law.

5. In conclusion, smoking is dangerous.

6. There are three reasons why we do not need a ring road round the town.

7. After that the protesters moved to the city walls.

8. So, red has suggested danger for many years.

9. Is reading cool?

10. Moreover, the town does not need another supermarket.

Varying sentences

Objective: S11

Vary the structure of sentences within paragraphs to lend pace, variety and emphasis.

Teaching point:

If sentences in a paragraph are structured in the same way, the writing may become dull. Variation helps to hold interest. Different sentence structures and types effect the reader in different ways.

What you will need:
OHT or copymasters plus set of whiteboards.

Time:
5 - 10 minutes

Activity:

- Increasingly, pupils need to be able to read as writers ~ looking at quality writing, identifying how the writer has gained effects and then trying these out in their own writing.

- This activity has three parts

  a. Is a simple analysis of passage a, focusing upon why the first passage is dull, e.g. sentences all same length, sounds staccato, etc.

  b. Analyse passage b, identifying the strategies the writer uses to create suspense.

  c. Quick-fire sentence construction on whiteboards ~ you call out an instruction and the class has 10-15 seconds to make a sentence, e.g.

  Short and dramatic sentence.

  Question used in story.

  Descriptive sentence using darkness to build tension.

  Exclamation for impact, etc.

Check whiteboards, in activity c, for basic punctuation.

Challenge: Use the list of stylistic features to write your own paragraph similar to b.

What has been taught:
- Effective writers control and vary sentences for effect.

Varying sentences

a. It was dark. The road was quiet. Nothing moved. Sara waited. Then she ran. She shot past the house. She rushed. She got to the end of the road. She was relieved.

b. It was quite dark and the road was silent. Nothing moved. Sara waited under the lime trees by the post-box. Could anybody see her? She peered up the empty road, scanning the windows, the front gardens, the shadowy lawns. Nothing. Taking a deep breath, Sara darted down the road. Without hesitation, she dashed down the pavement, tucking into the shadows wherever she could. Just as the end of the road came into sight, she heard a front door open. Light spilled onto the road. She froze.

Style in information texts

Objective: S13a

Revise the stylistic features of information texts, which maintain the use of the present tense and the third person, organise and links information clearly; incorporate examples.

Teaching point:

Reminder of the basic structure/features of information texts (called 'report writing' at key stage 2).

What you will need:
Copymasters and a class set of whiteboards.

Time:
As you require

Activity:

- The task (which could be spread over a number of days) is to:

    a. reassemble the paragraphs into the correct order;

    b. label them, according to their function;

    c. identify the key stylistic features.

- When thinking about the style of a passage it may help to direct the class to look at the audience and purpose, the words and sentences used plus anything else about the presentation.

- Ask the class what they know about 'report writing'.

Challenge: same activity but within a short time span.

What has been taught:
1. Information (or 'report') texts are structured as follows:
    a. Introduction ~ introduces the reader to the subject ~ basic definition/classification.
    b. More technical/detailed description.
    c. Sequence of paragraphs that provides information, e.g. qualities, function, habits, behaviour, etc.
    d. Ending ~ often relating subject in a personal way to the reader.
2. The most common key word and sentence features include:
    a. Mainly written in present tense.
    b. Usually non-chronological.
    c. Focus on generic participants.
    d. Some specific/technical detail.
    e. Simple and compound sentences for clarity.
    f. Questions used to interest reader.
    g. Use of sub-headings.
    h. Connectives used to order points.
    i. Use of illustrations, diagrams, etc.

Style in information texts

Most of us know about frogs. Not many are aware that a disease has been killing this well~known creature. If we are not careful this loved amphibian might become a rarity.

Most of us know that frogs lay their eggs in the Spring in a large lump of frogspawn. The young develop and hatch out as tadpoles. These wriggle around, steadily transforming their shape into a miniature frog.

Frogs are amphibians. That means that they can live in both water and land.

The frogs found in the British Isles are a greeny-brown colour. They have long back legs which they use for jumping and swimming. In other countries frogs come in all shapes, colours and sizes ~ including bright red, yellow and green! There are over 3,000 types of frogs. They all have moist, soft skins. One interesting fact about frogs is that they partly breathe through their skin.

They are found all over the world. In the main they live near still water, where they feed and have their young. Some types of frog are quite shy and hide during the day. In this way they can hide themselves from any predators. In this country, for instance, many frogs get eaten by grass snakes or herons.

Style in recounts

Objective: S13b

Revise the stylistic features of recounts, which maintain the use of the past tense, clear chronology and temporal connectives.

Teaching point:

Reminder of the basic structure/features of recounts.

What you will need:
Copymasters and a class set of whiteboards

Time:
As you require

Activity:

- The tasks are to:

    a. Fill in the missing paragraph, using the same style.

    b. Identify the overall structure.

    c. Identify the key stylistic features.

- When thinking about the style of a passage it may help to direct the class to look at the audience and purpose, the words and sentences used plus anything else about the presentation.

- Ask the class what they know about 'recounts'.

Challenge: list examples (diary, autobiography, 'true stories' in magazines).

What has been taught:
1. Recounts are structured as follows:
   a. Opening ~ that sets the scene, usually mentioning when, who, where, what and why.
   b. Events paragraphed in chronological order.
   c. Closing ~ often giving an overall personal comment about what happened.
2. The most common key word and sentence features include:
   a. Mainly written in past tense.
   b. Usually chronological.
   c. Uses time connectives, e.g. first, next, after lunch, later that day, etc.
   d. Focus on individuals, e.g. we, I, Mum, etc.
   e. Might be supported by personal documents, e.g. letters, photos, maps, etc.

Badger Key Stage 3 Literacy Starters

First thing in the morning we set out for the big shopping center in Bristol.

My Dad drove us down the motorway so we got to Bristol pretty quickly. At the centre we all piled out and made out way in. Everyone wanted to go in different directions so we split up.

Shelly and I decided to go to the clothes shop and look at the bangles. I've got to get something for Sam's birthday, so we spent ages there. I got her a few things which will just have to do!

After that we made our way back to where we had planned to meet. Once we were all together we went in for a Big Mac. I was starving! I could have eaten two but Derek said that I would blow up like a balloon if I did. The cheek!

Once we had eaten ...

Later that afternoon we drove home. It had been a great trip ~ exhausting but worth it. Now I just have to find some paper to wrap Sam's stuff up and I'm home and dry.

Style in explanations

Objective: S13
Revise the stylistic features of explanation texts, which maintain the use of the present tense and impersonal voice, and link points clearly.

Teaching point:
Reminder of the structure/features of explanations.

What you will need:
Copymasters and whiteboards.

Time:
As you require

Activity:

- The tasks are to:

  1. Annotate the style of the passage.

  2. Label the function of each paragraph.

  When thinking about the style of a passage it may help to direct the class to look at the audience and purpose, the words and sentences used plus anything else about the presentation.

- Ask the class what they know about 'explanations'.

Challenge: Jot down three pieces of advice for anyone writing explanatory texts.

What has been taught:
1. Explanation texts are structured as follows:
   a. Introduction ~ introduces the reader to the subject.
   b. Sequence of paragraphs that provides a series of logical steps explaining how or why something occurs.
   c. Ending ~ once explanation is complete ~ possible general comment.
2. The most common key word and sentence features include:
   a. Mainly written in simple present tense.
   b. Connectives that signal time, e.g. then, next, etc.
   c. Causal connectives, e.g. because, so this causes.
   d. Some specific/technical detail.
   e. Use of sub-headings, illustrations, diagrams, etc.

Style in explanations

The Water Cycle

Most of us take water for granted. We turn on the tap and out it pours.

However, if you travel to hotter parts of the world you will know that water is precious. Although the world is covered by vast oceans, only 1% is drinkable ~ the rest is seawater. This small amount of freshwater keeps living creatures and plants alive. Luckily it is constantly recycled through what is known as 'the water cycle'.

Here is how it works.

The heat from the sun blasts down at the earth. This evaporates some of the water from the oceans, ponds and rivers. The evaporated water rises as 'water vapour'.

As the water vapour rises upwards it gets colder. It condenses into droplets of water. Up in the air billions of tiny droplets come together to form clouds. The more droplets that form together, the heavier the clouds become.

When the water in the clouds has formed into quite large droplets it becomes heavy. This causes the larger droplets to fall ~ as rain. So, down it falls, back into the oceans, lakes, ponds and rivers.

This miraculous process is continually happening without us being aware of it. It is nature's very own recycling process. Nothing is wasted! Perhaps we should be like nature ~ don't waste water. It is precious.

Style in instructions

Objective: S13

Revise the stylistic features of instructions, which are helpfully sequenced and signposted, deploy imperative verbs and provide clear guidance.

Teaching point:

Reminder of the structure/features of instructions.

What you will need:
Copymasters and a set of whiteboards.

Time:
As you require

Activity:

- The task is to:

    a. decide which of the 3 sets of instructions is best ~ order them and give reasons.

    b. work out basic structure.

    c. identify the key stylistic features.

- When thinking about the style of a passage it may help to direct the class to look at the audience and purpose, the words and sentences used plus anything else about the presentation.

- Ask the class what they know about instructions.

Challenge: list when instructions are used in everyday life.

What has been taught:
1. Instruction texts are structured as follows:
    a. Introduction ~ states what has to be achieved.
    b. Equipment needed.
    c. Sequenced steps to achieve goal.
    d. Ending ~ perhaps a test, evaluation or presentational suggestion.
2. The most common key word and sentence features include:
    a. Mainly written in imperative.
    b. Chronological ~ first, next, after that, etc.
    c. Use of numbers, alphabet, bullet points.
    d. Colon and commas in a list.
    e. Focus on general rather than named participants.
    f. Use of illustrations, diagrams, etc.

1. Juggling

    Get three juggling balls but start with only two. Throw one up and catch it with the other hand. Keep this going for a bit. Then when the first ball is at the top of the arc throw up the next in the opposite direction. Once you can do this include the third ball. Keep practising.

2. How to juggle

    What you need: 3 juggling balls and some space!
    What you *do:*
    - Throw one ball from the right hand up in the air and catch it with the left.
    - Keep practising this move back and forwards.
    - When you are confident add in a second ball.
    - To do this wait till the first is at the top of the arc.
    - Then throw up the other ball in the opposite direction.
    - Try to keep the balls going backwards and forwards.
    - When you are ready add in the third.

3. How to juggle

    Juggling is great fun, entertaining and relaxing. Follow these instructions to get you going.

    What you need: 3 juggling balls and plenty of space!
    What you *do:*
    - Start with one ball.
    - Get used to throwing it smoothly, in an arc, from one hand to the other.
    - When you are confident then take the 2nd ball.
    - Hold a ball in each hand and throw one up in an arc.
    - As it reaches the top of the arc throw up the second.
    - Keep practising this until you can easily and smoothly catch both balls.
    - Now add in the third ball.

    Keep practising ~ it's worth it!

Style in persuasive writing

Objective: S13e

Revise the stylistic features of persuasion, which emphasises key points and articulates logical links in the argument.

Teaching point:

The structure and stylistic features of persuasion.

What you will need:
Copymasters and a class set of whiteboards.

Time:
As you require

Activity:

- The task is to annotate the example, focusing on:

    a. Who wrote this and why?

    b. What is the basic structure?

    c. What are the key stylistic features?

- When thinking about the style of a passage it may help to direct the class to look at the audience and purpose, the words and sentences used plus anything else about the presentation.

- Ask the class what they know about persuasive writing.

Challenge: Give three instances where someone might be telling the whole truth when using persuasive writing.

What has been taught:
- Persuasive writing can be structured as follows:
    a. Introduce reader to the viewpoint.
    b. Supporting points of argument, plus evidence and elaboration.
    c. Possible dealing with counter-arguments.
    d. Ending ~ reiterating opening position.

The most common key word and sentence features include:
    a. Usually present tense.
    b. Often focus on generic participants.
    c. Simple and compound sentences for clarity.
    d. Complex sentences to give reasons and argue points.
    e. Questions used to interest reader.
    f. Exclamations to force home points.
    g. Use of sub-headings.
    h. Logical connectives, e.g. therefore, however.
    i. Possible use of illustrations, diagrams, etc.

Style in persuasive writing

Most of us will have seen the bulletins on the television of poverty in the third world. But how many of us have actually given money to charity or helped in any way? This situation cannot continue.

In this country we are lucky. There is a roof over our heads, food in our bellies and water to drink. We can educate our children so that they learn to read and write. There are places to go for entertainment. We may not always feel it but in comparison to poorer countries we are wealthy. For instance, if fall sick then we will be looked after by a free health service. If we become unemployed then we are still supported.

Surely, in a so-called civilized society we should be able to support those across the world who are less fortunate. Over the years we have seen so many pictures of poor children, thin as sticks, grubbing on the ground for a grain of wheat to eat. Maybe we have seen to many pictures and therefore no longer take any notice.

When you next take a sip of water or pick up a hot chip just pause. Pause before you drink or eat. Somewhere across the world there are others dying because they cannot drink. They cannot eat. They have no money, no home. Let us not ignore this state of affairs. If we all contribute, even a small amount, then we can help more and more people. In the end, if you pause and think, you will know that you have no choice.

Guess the style

Objective: S13

Revise the stylistic features of non-fiction texts.

What you will need:
Copymasters or OHT
and a class set
of whiteboards.

Time:
Up to 10 minutes

Teaching point:

This revision from key stage 2 focuses on identifying typical
different stylistic features (poetry, narrative types as well as
non-fiction are included).

Activity:

- The task is to label each sentence, deciding what type of text it came from and to give at least one reason.

- Is there anything about the words used (technical vocabulary, certain connectives, formal language, particular use of verbs or adjectives, etc)?

- Is there anything about the sentences used (use of passive, past or present tense, first or third person, short or long sentences, imperative, etc)?

- Is there anything else particular about the presentation of the text (use of bullet points, headings, diagrams, etc)?

This task might be helpful in a run up to a sequence of work on non-fiction texts, to tune
pupils back into what they have previously covered at key stage 2.

Challenge: Give two or three reasons.

What has been taught:
- Writing used for different situations calls for different styles.

Guess the style

Label each sentence ~ what type of writing is this? How do you know?

1. The rattlesnake carries a deadly poison in its fangs.

2. The balloon rises because the hot air is lighter than the cold.

3. On the other hand, some people believe that fish do not feel pain therefore it is not cruel to kill them.

4. Finally, light the blue touch paper and stand well clear.

5. The wind shreds the reeds.

6. Last Wednesday I went to see my Gran.

7. Tom grabbed the handle and turned it with all his force.

8. The main reason why smoking is dangerous, must be the undeniable force of all the medical proof that demonstrates the dangers.

9. The boy rode for a day, he rode for a night, he rode for a year and a day.

10. Tick Tocks keep you cool ~ why not buy one now?

Speech into writing

Objective: S16

Investigate differences between spoken and written language structures, e.g. hesitation in speech.

Teaching point:

Spoken language varies considerably to written language because it is usually supported by an immediate context.

What you will need:
Copymasters.

Time:
5 minutes

Activity:

- Read through the first mini dialogue and its written version.

- Discuss and list differences on a checklist.

- As a class work on the second mini dialogue, translating it into written language, e.g.

  Tammy turned to her mother, "Have you read it?" Mrs Jameson continued to stare at the map. They were thoroughly lost.
  "Mmmm," she responded, not even looking up, "Yeah." Tammy put the book down.
  "I loved the end," she said dreamily, not caring that her mother was not really listening.

- Add any extra points to the checklist.

- The class work rapidly through the third mini-dialogue, translating it into written language.

- End by adding any further points to the checklist.

Check basic punctuation.

Challenge: continue the passage.

What has been taught:
- Some key differences between spoken and written language are:
    - explain context (where, when, what, how);
    - use names;
    - complete sentences;
    - speech verbs to indicate how things are said;
    - describe actions and events;
    - suggest how characters feel, e.g. adverbs;
    - make meanings more explicit,
      e.g. it = homework.

1. Hi'ya. Have you got the homework? No.

   Just then, I ran into Solly. "Hi'ya," he shouted. I waved back to him.
   "Have you got the homework?" I asked. To my dismay he shook his head.
   "No," he muttered dismally.

2. Read it? Mmmm, yeah. loved the end.

3. Er, pass um. This? Ta.

Using formal language

Objective: S15
Vary the formality of language in speech and writing to suit different circumstances.

Teaching point:
Using formal language depends on the audience and purpose. It differs in several ways from informal.

What you will need:
Copymasters.

Time:
5 minutes

Activity:

- Read through the first pair of sentences on the copymasters.

- Discuss each, deciding on suitability with reference to where (kitchen, playground, police court, etc) and with whom (friends, family, important guests, etc). Note variation in formality.

- As a class translate the next sentence from formal into informal.

- The task is then for the class to translate the next two sentences from formal into informal and the final two from informal into formal.

Check basic punctuation.

This activity could be used over several days ~ focusing on shifting from informal to formal and then the other way round.

Challenge: Invent formal sentences for the class to translate.

What has been taught:
- the use of formal language depends on where you are and whom you are with ~ more formal language might use:
  - More complex sentences.
  - Possible use of passive.
  - Few contractions such as 'can't'.
  - Specialist language.
  - No slang or chatty terms.
  - Address listener as 'you', etc.

Using formal language

1. Discuss:

   "Let's have one..."

   or

   "Excuse me, would you be kind enough to pass me the file marked 'Nuclear'?"

2. Translate from informal into formal:

   "Oi, gerroff!"

3. Translate from informal to formal and formal to informal:

   • "You got the doobrey?"

   • "It's in the motor, you dummy!"

   • "Police have begun to search buildings on the far side of Newcastle."

   • "In the event of fire, customers are required to make their way calmly to the fire exit and leave in an orderly fashion."

Standard English

Objective: S17

Use standard English consistently in formal situations and in writing.

Teaching point:

Changing local dialect into standard English.

What you will need:
Copymasters

Time:
5 minutes

Activity:

- Read through the copymaster and the class should rapidly jot down the changes needed to turn the sentences into standard English.

- As a class discuss the need to vary language in speech or writing, depending on the occasion ~ the audience and purpose.

Check basic punctuation.

Challenge: Make a list of any local ways of talking that are different to standard English.

What has been taught:
- Standard English uses certain forms.

Standard English

She was dead lucky.

He was frit.

I seen her.

She drank real fast.

She were at the park.

They was down the pool.

I want them books.

I didn't say nowt to nobody.

That is the pen what I bought.

I buyed it, look.

You'se all coming?

That bain't be true.

It's true, right?

There's some pens over there.

He likes footie, he does.

Old and new

Objective: S18

Identify specific ways sentence structure and punctuation are different in older texts.

Teaching point:

Language constantly changes.

What you will need:
Copymasters.

Time:
5 - 10 minutes

Activity:

The task is to place the 6 extracts on a time line ~ numbering from 1 to 6, with 1 as the earliest sentence.

Key:

1. Sixteenth century ~ Shakespeare (*The Tempest*).

2. Twenty-first century (text message).

3. Old English (Lord's prayer).

4. Eighteenth century ~ Johnathan Swift (*Proposal for improving English*).

5. Middle English (*Lord's Prayer*).

6. Twentieth century '60s' speak.

- Discuss specific differences.

- Make quick list of common expressions that were not in use when they were in primary school ~ text message expressions or email terms are useful examples.

Challenge: Write up the following words ~ guess which country they originated from ~ use a dictionary to find origins: garage (French), potato (Spanish), shampoo (India), dollar (Dutch), anorak (Eskimo), coffee (Turkey).

What has been taught:
- Language constantly changes, both in sentence structure, use of words and vocabulary.

Old and new

1. The clouds methought would open.

2. BTW G2G 2 LDN.

3. Faeder ure
    Þu þe eart on heofonum

4. There is another Sett of Men who have contributed very much
    to the spoiling of the English Tongue; I mean the poets.

5. Oure fadir that art in heuenys,
    Halewid be thy name.

6. Let's get the bread from the cool cat.

Improving style ~ alliteration

Objective:

Using alliteration to make sentences memorable.

What you will need:
A set of whiteboards.

Time:
2 - 5 minutes

Teaching point:

Alliteration creates a memorable sound effect that draws the reader's attention.

Activity:

- Read aloud the following two sentences ~ class jot down what is special about them. If needs be, prompt by asking them to listen to the sounds in the words:

  Best British Burgers ~ Buy now.

  The silver salmon swam silently.

- Somebody will notice the alliteration. Explain that this is the repetition of the same sound (not necessarily letters).

- Alliteration draws attention to the phrase or sentence, so it is often used in advertising as it can make a slogan memorable. Design slogans built around the following words, using alliteration: carrots, chocolate, kite.

- For example ~ Clever Clive's Kites climb high.

- Invent descriptive sentences built around the following words, using alliteration: bees, whale, tiny.
  e.g. The busy bees buzzed bravely by Barbar's burnt bald patch.

- Further possible activities ~ invent an alliterative alphabet (as many letters as you can in 5 minutes) built around animals or names, e.g. an ant ate an apple, a bear bought a bus, etc. Or awful Arthur, big Boris, clever Clive, etc.

Check for basic punctuation.

This activity can be used over a week, slogans on day 1, descriptive sentences day 2, alphabets days 3 ~ 5.

Challenge: Invent further slogans or sentences in the given time.

What has been taught:
- Reminder about alliteration being useful for making sentences more memorable.

Improving style ~ similes

Objective:

Use similes to create a stronger picture for the reader.

Teaching point:

Similes liken one thing to another.

What you will need:
A set of whiteboards.

Time:
2 - 5 minutes

Activity:

- Read aloud the following two sentences ~ class jot down what special effect the writer is using:
  - The moon rose like a golden balloon.
  - His fingers were slim as chicken bones.

- Revisit what the class know about similes and make a quick 'reminder'. Then play the following quick-fire games:

- Create a simile using 'like' for the following (it helps to think of the shape):
  The sun looked like? The crescent moon looked like? The flame flickered like?
  The windows were like? The snake was like?

- Complete the following: as quick as . . . . . . , as slow as . . . . . . , as dark as . . . . . . ,
  as thin as . . . . . . , as calm as . . . .

- In this game you are given a simile, e.g. as slow as a slug. You then have to exaggerate the simile further, e.g. as slow as a slug stuck in super-glue.

  - as tall as the post office tower
  - as fast as a jet
  - as hot as pepper
  - as small as an ant
  - as thin as a pencil

- Invent new similes for these well-known ones: as black as coal, as thin as a rake, as white as snow, as hot as mustard, as bold as brass.

Challenge: Use similes in your own story writing.

What has been taught:
- Reminder about invention and use of similes to create pictures for the reader.

Improving style ~ metaphors

Objective:

Using metaphors to make writing more powerful.

Teaching point:

Metaphor creates powerful pictures for the reader.

What you will need:
A set of whiteboards.

Time:
2 - 5 minutes

Activity:

- Read aloud the following two sentences ~ what is special about them?
  - *The sea is a hungry dog.*
  - *The moon is a thin smile.*

- Look at the difference between metaphor (writing about one thing as if it was another) and simile.

- Transform these similes into metaphors (by missing out the 'like'):
  - *The sky is like a table cloth.*
  - *The fields are like a quilt.*

- Jot down ideas for a description of a place by listing 5 things you can see on the left-hand side of the board (walls, taxis, pavement, etc) and 5 vegetables or fruit (avocado, lettuce, grapes, etc):
  In our town ~ / The walls are grapes / Piled up high, / The taxis are avocados /
  Bustling along, / The pavement is a lettuce / Spread out beneath my feet…

- Create a metaphoric alphabet by turning people into animals, e.g.
  Ann is an antelope, leaping.
  Bill is badger, blundering along.
  Coram is a cat, sneaking along a wall.

- Select a person. Turn them into ~ a place, an object, an animal, a fruit, a colour, a feeling, a day of the week, a number, an insect, etc. E.g.
  She is London city, bustling bright lights. / She is blue as the sea. / She is calm. /
  She is Monday, when the moon is out. / She is the luckiest number 7.
  She is a glow worm, bright at night, etc.

Check for basic punctuation.

Challenge: Collect metaphors from everyday speech, e.g. he is stone deaf.

What has been taught:
- Reminder about metaphor to make writing powerful.

Improving style ~ personification

Objective:

Using personification to make writing powerful.

Teaching point:

Personification creates powerful pictures in the reader's mind.

What you will need:
A set of whiteboards.

Time:
2 - 5 minutes

Activity:

- Read aloud the following two sentences ~ class jot down what special effect is being used:
  - The moon yawned.
  - The shadows shivered.

- Discuss 'personification' ~ a metaphorical device in which objects 'come alive'.

- Make a quick list of objects in the room (board, ohp, table, chair, window, etc).

- Make a quick list of verbs ~ but they must be verbs that describe human actions (yawn, sneeze, giggle, chatter, wink, run, etc).

- Quickfire writing ~ short sentences that bring the two lists together, e.g.
  In our classroom/The board yawns,/The tables chatter,/Chairs cross their legs,/The windows wink…

- Provide a few starters and the class have to extend the idea, e.g.
  The sea dozes
  becomes ~
  The sea dozes, sleeping deep beneath the warm skies.

- Try extending these ideas:
  - The trees whisper
  - The tables giggled
  - The wind howls

Check for basic punctuation.

Challenge: Find personification in any novel.

What has been taught:
- What has been taught: reminder about personification as a powerful writing technique.